M000206976

PLANNING
FOR THE

BATTLE
OF THE
BULGE

A Companion Workbook/Journal for
Winning the Battle of the Bulge

MARY ENGLUND MURPHY

Planning for the Battle of the Bulge
The Companion Workbook/Journal
for Winning the Battle of the Bulge
© 2006, by Mary Englund Murphy
Published by Looking Glass Press
10632 South Memorial Drive, Suite 126
Tulsa, Oklahoma 74133

All Rights Reserved. The text published in this book may not be reproduced, stored in any retrieval system, or transmitted in any form or by any means, electronic, mechanical, photocopying, recording, or otherwise, without the prior written permission of the publisher.

ISBN: 0-9778264-1-4

Scripture taken from the HOLY BIBLE, NEW INTERNATIONAL VERSION.
Copyright © 1973, 1978, 1984 International Bible Society.
Used by permission of Zondervan Bible Publishers.
and
The New King James Version.
Copyright © 1979, 1980, 1982 by Thomas Nelson, Inc.
Used by permission. All rights reserved.

Cover Design by Misenheimer Creative, Inc., www.misenheimer.com
Photography by Ann Miller, www.chase3000.com/pagesoftime
Edited by Melanie Rigney, www.editorforyou.com

Before beginning any new eating program consult a physician.

TABLE OF CONTENTS

Using Your Workbook/Journal

This workbook/journal is to record your thoughts, prayers, and insights into God's Word; it will be your personal chronicle of victory. In order to get the most out of this workbook/journal, read the entire book *Winning the Battle of the Bulge* before you begin. It will give you a complete overview of the program and a better understanding of the concept. Then, each week you will review one or two chapters in the book that correspond to that week's subject matter. For the greatest success and accountability, complete your workbook/journal each day.

Measurement/Weight Chart. Record your body measurements once a month. Always use the same tape measure to maintain accuracy. There will be times that you may not see a difference on the scale, but you will still be losing inches, especially if you are exercising regularly.

Weekly Memory Verses: Each week you will be given Scripture verses to commit to memory. These verses will help you throughout the week with your food battles.

Sunday, Day One: Complete each space in preparation for the coming week.

❖ *Date and Weight*: Weigh at least once per week (more often, if you prefer) at the same time of day for accurate loss or gain.
❖ *Weekly Overview*: Write down specific food battles you anticipate in the coming week such as a birthday party, a dinner date, or a church supper. By planning what you will eat at each event and the amount you will eat; you will have already won a victory!
❖ *Goals*: Write down your spiritual, mental and emotional, and physical goals. Break your long-term objectives into weekly short-term goals. Stretch yourself in each of these areas. Try to accomplish a little more each week.
❖ *Battle Buddy*: No soldier goes into battle alone; it is important to have a support system. You and your battle buddy will mutually pray for and encourage each other throughout the week. You will hold each other accountable by making regular contact. Record your battle buddy's telephone number, e-mail address, and any specific prayer needs including his or her weekly character quality.
❖ *Character Quality*: Prayerfully determine and record the character

quality you feel God wants to develop in you each week (patience, discipline, commitment, orderliness, diligence, honesty, self-control, etc), and the reason you chose it. This will be one of your greatest weekly challenges, but will give you strength for battle.

❖ *Prayer for the Week*: Record your prayer requests, thoughts, ideas, and concerns.

Monday, Day Two through Saturday, Day Seven: The format for these six days will be the same. Each day you will read Bible verses, answer questions, and record your personal insights. Use the Bible version with which you are most comfortable. Occasionally, a specific version is noted because I felt a particular word or phrase more clearly conveys the message.

The Bible is *not* a diet book, yet it has guidelines and principles that are applicable to healthy eating habits. Most Scripture references will not specifically refer to eating, but the principles may be applied to developing godly character with regard to eating and exercise.

❖ *Weight*: Record your weight if you opt to weigh daily.

❖ *Water*: Record your water intake as a reminder to keep your body hydrated.

❖ *Exercise*: Record what exercise you do and for how long. Try to exercise at least three times per week for thirty minutes.

❖ *Breakfast, Lunch, Dinner, Snacks*: Record *everything* you eat and drink (if the beverage contains calories). *Winning the Battle of the Bulge* is not a diet book and does not propose any specific diet plan. It is designed to help you renovate yourself spiritually, mentally and emotionally, and physically in order to live a healthy lifestyle. (Before you begin, ask your doctor for help in choosing a healthy eating and exercise plan.). Each meal or snack is a battle for most people; therefore, each evening, plan your food for the following day. You will more likely adhere to your plan if you write it out and commit to it in advance. If you wait until after a meal to record your food intake, you may find yourself eating more than you realize.

❖ *Battle Buddy*: Place a check in this space each time you pray for your battle buddy and each time you make contact with an encouraging word by phone, e-mail, note, or card.

❖ *Today's Scripture*: Read the Bible verses and answer each question in *your own words*. The questions are designed to help you search your heart and motives for honest answers that will promote a genuine, lasting change in your eating habits. Ask God to help you personally apply each verse to your battle of the bulge.

❖ *New Insights*: Record any new insights you gleaned from your Scripture reading or from your daily experiences.

❖ *Prayer for Today*: Write down your requests, struggles, and praises.

❖ *Victories/Defeats*: With an emphasis on character development, record your victories and defeats. Were you *diligent* to say no when you were offered a donut at the office? Did you keep your *focus* and pass up the dessert table at the church supper? Were you *faithful* to read today's Scripture and answer the questions? Did you *persevere* and exercise even when you didn't feel like it?

You are ready to begin your *Planning for the Battle of the Bulge* workbook/journal. May you find victory in Christ.

Mary Englund Murphy

Winning the Battle of the Bulge – Weight / Measurement Chart

Date											Yearly Total
Weight											
Bust											
Chest											
Right Arm											
Left Arm											
Waist											
Hips											
Buttocks											
Right Thigh											
Left Thigh											
Right Calf											
Left Calf											
Weekly Total											

ENLISTMENT: I WANT YOU!

"Therefore I run thus: not with uncertainty.
Thus I fight: not as one who beats the air.
But I discipline my body and bring it into subjection,
lest, when I have preached to others,
I myself should become disqualified."
1 Corinthians 9:26- 27

Week 1   *Enlistment*

Weekly memory verses: 1 Corinthians 9:26-27

Review chapters one (*The Battle*) and two (*Enlistment: I Want You!*) in the book *Winning the Battle of the Bulge*.

Enlistment is your first step toward victory in your battle of the bulge. The word "enlistment" implies commitment. When you enlist in God's army, you are committing to obey your commander in chief the Lord Jesus Christ, adopt his goals for your life, and make the changes in your life necessary to meet those goals.

Enlistment is *not* the same as salvation. Salvation is accepting God's free gift of eternal life by faith in Christ's death, burial, and resurrection as payment for your sins. Enlistment takes work and is a form of discipleship. You are making a choice to obediently follow Christ as your commander in chief. As a new recruit, you may not always know what to expect, but that's all right; take one day at a time, one battle at a time. Each day will bring new trials and tests, but you will be victorious in Christ as you are obedient to each new challenge.

In the spaces below, write your goals for the next twelve weeks:

Physically: _____

_____

_____

_____

_____

_____

Mentally/Emotionally: _____

_____

_____

_____

_____

_____

Spiritually: _____

_____

_____

_____

_____

_____

Week 1   *Sunday, Day 1*   *Enlistment*

Date: _____ **Weight:** _____

Weekly Overview (food battles you will you encounter this week):
Battle: _____ Day: _____
Battle plan: _____

Battle: _____ Day: _____
Battle plan: _____

Battle: _____ Day: _____
Battle plan: _____

Battle: _____ Day: _____
Battle plan: _____

Goals: _____
_____
_____

Battle Buddy: _____ **Phone:** _____
E-mail: _____ **Prayer needs:** _____
_____
_____

Character quality: _____
Why you need to develop this: _____
_____
_____
_____

Prayer for the week: _____
_____
_____
_____
_____
_____
_____

Week 1   *Monday*   *Enlistment*

Weight: _____ **Exercise:** _____ **Battle Buddy:** _____

Breakfast	Lunch	Dinner	Snacks
_____	_____	_____	_____
_____	_____	_____	_____
_____	_____	_____	**Water**
_____	_____	_____	_____

Today's Scripture: 2 Timothy 2:1-7 (NKJV)

Why does a soldier enlist in the army? _____
_____

What might enlistment entail? _____
_____
_____
_____

Why are you enlisting in the battle of the bulge? _____
_____
_____
_____

From where do you get understanding to fight your battle? _____
_____
_____

New insights: _____
_____
_____

Prayer for today: _____
_____
_____
_____

Victories/defeats today: _____
_____
_____

Week 1   *Tuesday*   *Enlistment*

Weight: _____   **Exercise**: _____   **Battle Buddy**: _____

Breakfast	Lunch	Dinner	Snacks
_____	_____	_____	_____
_____	_____	_____	_____
_____	_____	_____	_____
_____	_____	_____	**Water**
_____	_____	_____	_____

Today's Scripture: Repeat 2 Timothy 2:1-7 (NKJV)

Who has enlisted you as a soldier? _____

What hardships might you encounter in your battle? _____
_____
_____
_____

How has the world's view of weight loss affected you? _____
_____
_____
_____

What can you do today to please Christ, the one who enlisted you? _____
_____
_____
_____

New insights: _____
_____
_____

Prayer for today: _____
_____
_____
_____

Victories/defeats today: _____
_____
_____

Week 1   *Wednesday*   *Enlistment*

Weight: _____   **Exercise:** _____   **Battle Buddy:** _____

Breakfast	Lunch	Dinner	Snacks
_____	_____	_____	_____
_____	_____	_____	_____
_____	_____	_____	_____
_____	_____	_____	**Water**
_____	_____	_____	_____

Today's Scripture: Joshua 1:9

Enlistment implies commitment. In the past, you probably committed to a diet plan. What are you committing to now? _____

_____

What is the difference? _____

_____

Why does it take strength and courage to be obedient? _____

_____

_____

In the past, what have you used to strengthen yourself to lose weight? _____

_____

_____

Why should you not be discouraged or afraid? _____

_____

_____

New insights: _____

_____

Prayer for today: _____

_____

_____

Victories/defeats today: _____

_____

_____

Week 1   **Thursday**   *Enlistment*

Weight: _____   **Exercise:** _____   **Battle Buddy:** _____

Breakfast	Lunch	Dinner	Snacks
_____	_____	_____	_____
_____	_____	_____	_____
_____	_____	_____	_____
_____	_____	_____	**Water**
_____	_____	_____	_____

Today's Scripture: 2 Peter 1:2-8

Where do you get all you need to fight your battle? _____
_____
_____

What will God's power do for you? _____
_____
_____

Of the virtues listed in verses five through seven, on which do you most need to work? _____
_____
_____

How will these virtues help you in your battle? _____
_____
_____

New insights: _____
_____
_____

Prayer for today: _____
_____
_____
_____

Victories/defeats today: _____
_____
_____

Week 1 　　　　　　　　*Friday* 　　　　　　　　*Enlistment*

Weight: _____ **Exercise**: _____ **Battle Buddy**: _____

Breakfast	**Lunch**	**Dinner**	**Snacks**
_____	_____	_____	_____
_____	_____	_____	_____
_____	_____	_____	_____
_____	_____	_____	**Water**
_____	_____	_____	_____

Today's Scripture: Romans 12:1-2

How might it please God to offer your body as a sacrifice to him? _____

_____

_____

_____

How have you conformed your thinking and actions to the world regarding weight loss? _____

_____

_____

_____

What can you do to transform your thinking to be more like God's? _____

_____

_____

_____

_____

New insights: _____

_____

_____

Prayer for today: _____

_____

_____

_____

Victories/defeats today: _____

_____

_____

Week 1   *Saturday*   *Enlistment*

Weight: _____   **Exercise:** _____   **Battle Buddy:** _____

Breakfast	Lunch	Dinner	Snacks
_____	_____	_____	_____
_____	_____	_____	_____
_____	_____	_____	**Water**
_____	_____	_____	_____
_____	_____	_____	

Today's Scripture: Philippians 4:8

What does the Apostle Paul instruct you to think about? _____
_____
_____

Which of these is the most difficult for you to think about and why? _____
_____
_____

How has wrong thinking affected your weight-loss efforts? _____
_____
_____
_____

As an enlisted soldier, how should your thinking change? _____
_____
_____

New insights: _____
_____
_____

Prayer for today: _____
_____
_____
_____

Victories/defeats today: _____
_____
_____

BOOT CAMP:
YOU'RE IN THE ARMY NOW!

Lord, you have heard the desire of the humble;
You will prepare their heart.
Psalm 10:17

Week 2   *Boot Camp*

Weekly memory verse: Psalm 10:17

Read chapter three (*Boot Camp: You're in the Army Now!*) in the book *Winning the Battle of the Bulge: It's Not Just About the Weight*.

A successful soldier is trained during boot camp in every area—mind, will, body, and emotions. Some recruits fail because boot camp requires changes they don't want to make. Most dieters fail because they want an easy way to lose weight and aren't willing to change behavior patterns. After each discipline listed below, note how you might make a change in your own life.

Baring yourself before others: _____

_____

New purpose: _____

_____

New eating habits: _____

_____

New goals: _____

_____

Daily exercise: _____

_____

Accountability: _____

_____

Structure: _____

_____

Obedience: _____

_____

Giving up your rights/personal pleasures: _____

_____

New authority: _____

_____

New identity: _____

_____

Avoiding distractions: _____

_____

Week 2   *Sunday, Day 1*   *Enlistment*

Date: _____ **Weight**: _____

Weekly Overview (food battles you will you encounter this week):
Battle: _____ Day: _____
Battle plan: _____

Battle: _____ Day: _____
Battle plan: _____

Battle: _____ Day: _____
Battle plan: _____

Battle: _____ Day: _____
Battle plan: _____

Goals: _____
_____
_____

Battle Buddy: _____ **Phone**: _____
E-mail: _____ **Prayer needs**: _____
_____
_____

Character quality: _____
Why you need to develop this: _____
_____
_____
_____

Prayer for the week: _____
_____
_____
_____
_____
_____
_____

Week 2   *Monday*   *Boot Camp*

Weight: _____   **Exercise:** _____   **Battle Buddy:** _____

Breakfast	Lunch	Dinner	Snacks
_____	_____	_____	_____
_____	_____	_____	_____
_____	_____	_____	_____
_____	_____	_____	**Water**
_____	_____	_____	_____

Today's Scripture: Psalm 144:1-2

God will prepare you to fight your weight battle. With insight from chapter three, answer the following questions for today and tomorrow.

What fears and emotions are you experiencing? _____
_____
_____

How can you identify with Christ? _____
_____

What kind of loneliness might you experience in your battle? _____
_____
_____

What personal freedoms do you need to relinquish? _____
_____
_____

New insights: _____
_____
_____

Prayer for today: _____
_____
_____
_____

Victories/defeats today: _____
_____
_____

Week 2   *Tuesday*   *Boot Camp*

Weight: _____   Exercise: _____   Battle Buddy: _____

Breakfast	Lunch	Dinner	Snacks
_____	_____	_____	_____
_____	_____	_____	_____
_____	_____	_____	**Water**
_____	_____	_____	_____
_____	_____	_____	

Today's Scripture: Repeat Psalm 144:1-2

Have you ever allowed God to prepare you physically, mentally and emotionally, and spiritually *before* you began a diet? _____

How would preparations make a difference in your outcome? _____
_____
_____

In what ways do you need more structure and orderliness? _____
_____
_____

What is distracting you from your battle? _____
_____

In what way(s) do you need to be broken? _____
_____
_____

New insights: _____
_____
_____

Prayer for today: _____
_____
_____
_____

Victories/defeats today: _____
_____
_____

Week 2   *Wednesday*   *Boot Camp*

Weight: _____   **Exercise:** _____   **Battle Buddy:** _____

Breakfast	Lunch	Dinner	Snacks
_____	_____	_____	_____
_____	_____	_____	_____
_____	_____	_____	**Water**
_____	_____	_____	_____
_____	_____	_____	

Today's Scripture: Hebrews 12:1-2

Boot camp is about preparation. What specific areas of your life do you need to prepare for your battle of the bulge? _____
_____
_____

What have you allowed to entangle you regarding weight-loss? _____
_____
_____

What can you do to change? _____
_____
_____

On whom are you to focus? _____

What can you do to improve your focus? _____
_____
_____

New insights: _____
_____
_____

Prayer for today: _____
_____
_____

Victories/defeats today: _____
_____
_____

Week 2   ***Thursday***   *Boot Camp*

Weight: _____   Exercise: _____   Battle Buddy: _____

Breakfast	Lunch	Dinner	Snacks
_____	_____	_____	_____
_____	_____	_____	_____
_____	_____	_____	_____
_____	_____	_____	**Water**
_____	_____	_____	_____

Today's Scripture: Proverbs 10:17

In what areas of your life do you exercise discipline? _____
_____
_____

How did you develop discipline in those areas? _____
_____
_____

In what areas have you been undisciplined in your battle of the bulge? _____
_____
_____

What consequences are you experiencing because you have ignored correction regarding weight loss? _____
_____
_____

New insights: _____
_____
_____

Prayer for today: _____
_____
_____
_____

Victories/defeats today: _____
_____
_____

Week 2   *Friday*   *Boot Camp*

Weight: _____   Exercise: _____   Battle Buddy: _____

Breakfast	Lunch	Dinner	Snacks
_____	_____	_____	_____
_____	_____	_____	_____
_____	_____	_____	**Water**
_____	_____	_____	_____
_____	_____	_____	

Today's Scripture: Colossians 1:10, 11

The Apostle Paul prayed that the Colossians would develop endurance and patience through God's power. How long do you usually endure after starting a diet? _____

_____

Have you ever taken time to develop godly character such as diligence, discipline, patience, endurance, and self-control *before* you tried to lose weight? _____

How will it help you if you begin to develop godly character before and while you begin to change your eating and exercise habits? _____

_____

_____

_____

_____

_____

_____

New insights: _____

_____

_____

Prayer for today: _____

_____

_____

_____

Victories/defeats today: _____

_____

_____

Week 2   *Saturday*   *Boot Camp*

Weight: _____   Exercise: _____   Battle Buddy: _____

Breakfast	Lunch	Dinner	Snacks
_____	_____	_____	_____
_____	_____	_____	_____
_____	_____	_____	_____
_____	_____	_____	**Water**
_____	_____	_____	_____

Today's Scripture: Psalm 51:16-17

Boot camp breaks a soldier so he will: learn to obey commands without question, work as one with fellow soldiers toward a common goal, give up his rights for the good of the final objective, and develop character. Can you think of other reasons?

_____

_____

_____

Are you truly "broken" before God about weight loss, or just disgusted with how you look? _____

Are you ready to be obedient in your eating and exercise? _____

How are you thinking differently than you did two weeks ago? _____

_____

_____

_____

New insights: _____

_____

_____

Prayer for today: _____

_____

_____

_____

Victories/defeats today: _____

_____

_____

WEEK THREE

RECOGNIZING YOUR ENEMY

Be self-controlled and alert. Your enemy the devil prowls around like a roaring lion, looking for someone to devour. Resist him, standing firm in the faith, because you know that your brothers throughout the world are undergoing the same kind of sufferings.
1 Peter 5:8-9

Week 3   *The Enemy*

Weekly memory verses: 1 Peter 5:8, 9

Review chapter four (*Recognizing Your Enemy*) in the book *Winning the Battle of the Bulge*.

Longtime dieters sometimes view food, their appetites, and even other people as their enemies. While circumstances, food, and people certainly have an effect on eating behavior and patterns, those things are not the primary enemies.

Satan is your enemy and he wants to attack every area of your life to get your focus off Christ. *He is your enemy because he is God's enemy.*

Satan wants you to be discouraged and give in to your selfish desires. God wants to build strength and godly character in your life so you will grow to be more like him each day.

Week 3   *Sunday, Day 1*   *The Enemy*

Date: _____ **Weight**: _____

Weekly Overview (food battles you will you encounter this week):
Battle: _____ Day: _____
Battle plan: _____

Battle: _____ Day: _____
Battle plan: _____

Battle: _____ Day: _____
Battle plan: _____

Battle: _____ Day: _____
Battle plan: _____

Goals: _____
_____
_____

Battle Buddy: _____ **Phone**: _____
E-mail: _____ **Prayer needs**: _____
_____
_____

Character quality: _____
Why you need to develop this: _____
_____
_____
_____

Prayer for the week: _____
_____
_____
_____
_____
_____
_____

Week 3   *Monday*   *The Enemy*

Weight: _____ **Exercise:** _____ **Battle Buddy:** _____

Breakfast	**Lunch**	**Dinner**	**Snacks**
_____	_____	_____	_____
_____	_____	_____	_____
_____	_____	_____	**Water**
_____	_____	_____	_____
_____	_____	_____	

Today's Scripture: John 8:44b and John 14:6

Who is the father of lies? _____

Who is truth? _____

What lies have you believed about yourself? _____
_____
_____

What lies have you believed about your weight loss? _____
_____
_____

What truths do you need to accept about yourself spiritually, mentally and emotionally, and physically? _____
_____
_____
_____

New insights: _____
_____
_____

Prayer for today: _____
_____
_____
_____

Victories/defeats today: _____
_____
_____

Week 3   *Tuesday*   *The Enemy*

Weight: _____   Exercise: _____   Battle Buddy: _____

Breakfast	**Lunch**	**Dinner**	**Snacks**
_____	_____	_____	_____
_____	_____	_____	_____
_____	_____	_____	_____
_____	_____	_____	**Water**
_____	_____	_____	_____

Today's Scripture: I Peter 5:8-11

Now that you know who your enemy is, what character qualities do you need to develop for your battle? _____
_____
_____

What will help you resist the enemy? _____
_____
_____

How can you stand firm in the faith? _____
_____
_____

Who gets the glory if you are obedient? _____

Who gets the glory with traditional dieting victories? _____
_____

New insights: _____
_____
_____

Prayer for today: _____
_____
_____

Victories/defeats today: _____
_____
_____

Week 3   *Wednesday*   *The Enemy*

Weight: _____   Exercise: _____   Battle Buddy: _____

Breakfast	Lunch	Dinner	Snacks
_____	_____	_____	_____
_____	_____	_____	_____
_____	_____	_____	_____
_____	_____	_____	**Water**
_____	_____	_____	_____

Today's Scripture: Ephesians 6:10-13

Where should you get your power and strength to fight your battle? _____
_____
_____

How can you get that strength and power? _____
_____

Where have you turned in the past for power and strength to fight your battle?
_____
_____
_____

Why is Satan such a difficult enemy to fight? _____
_____
_____
_____
_____

New insights: _____
_____
_____

Prayer for today: _____
_____
_____

Victories/defeats today: _____
_____
_____

Week 3   *Thursday*   *The Enemy*

Weight: _____   **Exercise:** _____   **Battle Buddy:** _____

Breakfast	Lunch	Dinner	Snacks
_____	_____	_____	_____
_____	_____	_____	_____
_____	_____	_____	_____
_____	_____	_____	**Water**
_____	_____	_____	_____

Today's Scripture: James 4:1-6

Satan is your enemy, but he does not make you overeat or eat unhealthy food. From where do battles and wars come? _____
_____
_____

Food is a gift from God. Is it wrong to eat for pleasure? _____

When does it become wrong? _____
_____
_____

How do these verses apply to your former eating habits? _____
_____
_____
_____
_____

New insights: _____
_____
_____

Prayer for today: _____
_____
_____
_____

Victories/defeats today: _____
_____
_____

Week 3   *Friday*   *The Enemy*

Weight: _____   Exercise: _____   Battle Buddy: _____

Breakfast	Lunch	Dinner	Snacks
_____	_____	_____	_____
_____	_____	_____	_____
_____	_____	_____	_____
_____	_____	_____	**Water**
_____	_____	_____	_____

Today's Scripture: James 4:7-10

Satan will flee when you resist him, but what must you do? _____
_____
_____

Regarding your eating habits:

How have you not submitted to God? _____
_____
_____
_____

How have you not been pure? _____
_____

How have you been double-minded? _____
_____
_____

New insights: _____
_____
_____

Prayer for today: _____
_____
_____
_____

Victories/defeats today: _____
_____
_____

Week 3   *Saturday*   *The Enemy*

Weight: _____   Exercise: _____   Battle Buddy: _____

Breakfast	Lunch	Dinner	Snacks
_____	_____	_____	_____
_____	_____	_____	_____
_____	_____	_____	**Water**
_____	_____	_____	_____
_____	_____	_____	

Today's Scripture: Review this week's Scripture

Battles cannot be won if you don't understand your enemy's strengths and weaknesses. Based on this week's Scripture, what have you learned about the enemy that will help you win your battle? _____

_____

_____

_____

_____

_____

_____

_____

_____

_____

_____

_____

_____

New insights: _____

_____

_____

Prayer for today: _____

_____

_____

_____

Victories/defeats today: _____

_____

_____

PLANNING FOR BATTLE

*Praise be to the LORD my Rock, who trains my
hands for war, my fingers for battle.
Psalm 144: 1*

*Wisdom is supreme; therefore get wisdom. Though
it cost all you have, get understanding.
Proverbs 4:7*

Week 4   *Planning For Battle*

Weekly memory verses: Psalm 144:1 and Proverbs 4:7b

Review chapters five (*Planning for Battle*) and seventeen (*Battling Tips*) in the book *Winning the Battle of the Bulge.*

Imagine yourself at war, a real war with real guns, tanks, ammunition, a battlefield, an enemy, your commander, fellow soldiers, and most of all a goal—a purpose for fighting the war. Each day for the rest of your life you will be fighting in this war—sometimes in minor skirmishes, sometimes in bloody battles, and sometimes in surprise attacks. Sometimes you will lose, but most of the time you will win because *you* have the most powerful weapons, the best commander, and you are learning to be obedient in truth, integrity, discipline, and diligence. Sometimes you will feel like giving up, but you won't because the struggle is worthwhile, and you don't want the enemy to win.

Your battle of the bulge is a real battle that needs planning and preparation. Don't wait until you are standing in a buffet line, sitting at the dinner table, or pulling into a fast food restaurant. It is important to plan what to eat, but you should also plan what *not* to eat, and then commit to follow your plan.

Sometimes you will experience surprise attacks (doughnuts at the office, an impromptu luncheon invitation, etc). Plan in advance what you will do in those situations.

This week, after reading each day's Scripture, you will be presented with a hypothetical eating situation; make a plan for each battle.

Week 4   *Sunday, Day 1*   *Battle Plans*

Date: _____ **Weight**: _____

Weekly Overview (food battles you will you encounter this week):
Battle: _____ Day: _____
Battle plan: _____

Battle: _____ Day: _____
Battle plan: _____

Battle: _____ Day: _____
Battle plan: _____

Battle: _____ Day: _____
Battle plan: _____

Goals: _____
_____
_____

Battle Buddy: _____ **Phone**: _____
E-mail: _____ **Prayer needs**: _____
_____
_____

Character quality: _____
Why you need to develop this: _____
_____
_____
_____

Prayer for the week: _____
_____
_____
_____
_____
_____
_____

Week 4   *Monday*   *Battle Plans*

Weight: _____   **Exercise:** _____   **Battle Buddy:** _____

Breakfast	Lunch	Dinner	Snacks
_____	_____	_____	_____
_____	_____	_____	_____
_____	_____	_____	**Water**
_____	_____	_____	_____

Today's Scripture: Psalm 25:1-5

When you live (give) your life for the Lord, what five things will he do for you according to these verses?

1) _____

_____

2) _____

_____

3) _____

_____

4) _____

_____

5) _____

_____

It's 3:00 p.m. and you're starving. Make a battle plan for your daily snack time.

_____

New insights: _____

_____

Prayer for today: _____

_____

Victories/defeats today: _____

_____

_____

Week 4   *Tuesday*   *Battle Plans*

Weight: _____   Exercise: _____   Battle Buddy: _____

Breakfast	Lunch	Dinner	Snacks
_____	_____	_____	_____
_____	_____	_____	_____
_____	_____	_____	_____
_____	_____	_____	**Water**
_____	_____	_____	_____

Today's Scripture: Psalm 31:1-5

Sometimes you will be battle weary. List everything God promises to do for you
when you take refuge in him. _____

_____

_____

_____

_____

_____

_____

_____

You're celebrating at your favorite restaurant. Make a battle plan. _____

_____

_____

_____

New insights: _____

_____

_____

Prayer for today: _____

_____

_____

_____

Victories/defeats today: _____

_____

_____

Week 4   *Wednesday*   *Battle Plans*

Weight: _____   Exercise: _____   Battle Buddy: _____

Breakfast	Lunch	Dinner	Snacks
_____	_____	_____	_____
_____	_____	_____	_____
_____	_____	_____	_____
_____	_____	_____	**Water**
_____	_____	_____	_____

Today's Scripture: 2 Samuel 2:1-7

God is preparing you for battle. He is your fortress, your stronghold, your deliverer, your shield, and your refuge. How is each of these evident in your life?

_____

_____

_____

_____

_____

_____

_____

_____

Your friends invite you to dinner and will be serving your favorite foods—including your favorite dessert. Make a battle plan. _____

_____

_____

_____

New insights: _____

_____

_____

Prayer for today: _____

_____

_____

_____

Victories/defeats today: _____

_____

_____

Week 4   *Thursday*   *Battle Plans*

Weight: _____   Exercise: _____   Battle Buddy: _____

Breakfast	Lunch	Dinner	Snacks
_____	_____	_____	_____
_____	_____	_____	_____
_____	_____	_____	_____
_____	_____	_____	**Water**
_____	_____	_____	_____

Today's Scripture: 1 Samuel 17:1-51

God fellowshipped with David in the fields, and David diligently practiced with his slingshot while protecting the flocks. When he faced Goliath he was prepared physically, mentally and emotionally, and spiritually. What situations in your life has God been using to prepare you to defeat the enemy?

_____
_____
_____
_____
_____
_____

You're invited to a birthday party, and you have no idea if there will be anything served besides cake. Make a battle plan. _____

_____
_____
_____

New insights: _____

_____
_____

Prayer for today: _____

_____
_____

Victories/defeats today: _____

_____
_____

Week 4   *Friday*   *Battle Plans*

Weight: _____   Exercise: _____   Battle Buddy: _____

Breakfast	Lunch	Dinner	Snacks
_____	_____	_____	_____
_____	_____	_____	_____
_____	_____	_____	**Water**
_____	_____	_____	
_____	_____	_____	_____

Today's Scripture: Genesis 25:27-34

Esau did not prepare extra food for his hunting trip. He allowed his hunger to control his mind, and he made a poor decision. Can you think of a time(s) when your stomach controlled your mind? _____
_____
_____
_____
_____

What character qualities did Esau lack? _____
_____

You're running late to church and have to feed the family at a fast-food restaurant. Make a battle plan. _____
_____
_____

New insights: _____
_____
_____

Prayer for today: _____
_____
_____
_____

Victories/defeats today: _____
_____
_____

Week 4   *Saturday*   *Battle Plans*

Weight: _____ **Exercise:** _____ **Battle Buddy:** _____

Breakfast	**Lunch**	**Dinner**	**Snacks**
_____	_____	_____	_____
_____	_____	_____	_____
_____	_____	_____	_____
_____	_____	_____	**Water**
_____	_____	_____	_____

Today's Scripture: John 6:1-14

The disciples were faced with a food dilemma. To whom did they turn for a plan?
_____

If Jesus can miraculously feed and satisfy the appetites of thousands of people, what can he do for you? _____
_____
_____
_____
_____
_____

It's two weeks till Christmas and you have five parties to attend. Make a battle plan. _____
_____
_____
_____

New insights: _____
_____
_____

Prayer for today: _____
_____
_____
_____

Victories/defeats today: _____
_____
_____

WEEK FIVE

UNDERSTANDING
WHY YOU FAIL

*I would have lost heart, unless I had believed that I would
see the goodness of the LORD in the land of the living.
Wait on the LORD; Be of good courage, and He shall
strengthen your heart; Wait, I say, on the LORD."
Psalm 27:13-14*

Week 5   *Why You Fail*

Weekly memory verses: Psalm 27:13-14

Review chapter six (*Understanding Why You Fail*) in the book *Winning the Battle of the Bulge.*

Discouragement is the simple answer for defeat and probably the biggest factor in giving up on a diet. You become discouraged, so you fail; you fail, so you become discouraged. It's a vicious circle that must stop, but how?

First, learn from your past mistakes; then, correct your thinking and behavior. You did not fail for one reason only; no doubt there were many reasons. While keeping a battle theme in mind, examine a few of the most common reasons for dieting failure.

You have not prepared yourself.
You are impatient and want instant results.
You do not have a plan.
You are fearful.
You are trying to focus on too many battles at one time
You think it's just too hard.
Your have a poor self-image and faulty perceptions.
You have unrealistic expectations.
You don't use the right weapons.
You reward yourself with food.
You focus on yourself instead of God.
You have developed bad habits.
You have wrong motives.
You overeat based on emotions rather than hunger.
  Anger
  Disappointment
  Loneliness
  Joy
  Fear
  Sadness
  Revenge

Week 5   *Sunday, Day 1*   *Why You Fail*

Date: _____ **Weight**: _____

Weekly Overview (food battles you will you encounter this week):
Battle: _____ Day: _____
Battle plan: _____

Battle: _____ Day: _____
Battle plan: _____

Battle: _____ Day: _____
Battle plan: _____

Battle: _____ Day: _____
Battle plan: _____

Goals: _____
_____
_____

Battle Buddy: _____ **Phone**: _____
E-mail: _____ **Prayer needs**: _____
_____
_____

Character quality: _____
Why you need to develop this: _____
_____
_____
_____

Prayer for the week: _____
_____
_____
_____
_____
_____
_____
_____

Week 5   *Monday*   *Why You Fail*

Weight: _____ **Exercise:** _____ **Battle Buddy:** _____

Breakfast	Lunch	Dinner	Snacks
_____	_____	_____	_____
_____	_____	_____	_____
_____	_____	_____	_____
_____	_____	_____	**Water**
_____	_____	_____	_____

Today's Scripture: Proverbs 15:22

To be victorious, you must understand why you failed in the past. This verse gives one reason why people fail. List the reasons you have failed at dieting. _____

_____

_____

_____

_____

_____

_____

_____

_____

_____

_____

_____

_____

New insights: _____

_____

_____

Prayer for today: _____

_____

_____

_____

Victories/defeats today: _____

_____

_____

Week 5   *Tuesday*   *Why You Fail*

Weight: _____   **Exercise:** _____   **Battle Buddy:** _____

Breakfast	Lunch	Dinner	Snacks
_____	_____	_____	_____
_____	_____	_____	_____
_____	_____	_____	**Water**
_____	_____	_____	_____
_____	_____	_____	

Today's Scripture: Philippians 4:12-13

Read yesterday's list of reasons for past fai lures. How can you turn each of those failures into victory in Christ? Be specific. _____

_____

_____

_____

_____

_____

_____

_____

_____

_____

_____

_____

_____

New insights: _____

_____

_____

Prayer for today: _____

_____

_____

_____

Victories/defeats today: _____

_____

_____

Week 5   *Wednesday*   *Why You Fail*

Weight: _____   Exercise: _____   Battle Buddy: _____

Breakfast	Lunch	Dinner	Snacks
_____	_____	_____	_____
_____	_____	_____	_____
_____	_____	_____	_____
_____	_____	_____	**Water**
_____	_____	_____	_____

Today's Scripture: 2 Samuel 11

King David put himself into a wrong situation with the wrong person. Sometimes we put ourselves into situations with people or places that present food temptations we're not able to handle. What are some of the situations that make it difficult for you to control what you eat? _____
_____
_____
_____
_____
_____

If you must be in those situations because of family, job, etc, what can you do to *prepare* yourself for the temptation? _____
_____
_____
_____

New insights: _____
_____
_____

Prayer for today: _____
_____
_____
_____

Victories/defeats today: _____
_____
_____

Week 5   *Thursday*   *Why You Fail*

Weight: _____ Exercise: _____ Battle Buddy: _____

Breakfast	Lunch	Dinner	Snacks
_____	_____	_____	_____
_____	_____	_____	_____
_____	_____	_____	**Water**
_____	_____	_____	_____
_____	_____	_____	

Today's Scripture: Philippians 2:12-14

Sometimes you fail because your goals are not clear. What are some of your past goals for losing weight? _____

_____

_____

_____

Who is working in you? _____ Have you grumbled about your weight-loss failures in the past? _____ In what ways? _____

_____

_____

_____

_____

How have your goals changed in the past four weeks? _____

_____

_____

New insights: _____

_____

_____

Prayer for today: _____

_____

_____

_____

Victories/defeats today: _____

_____

_____

Week 5   *Friday*   *Why You Fail*

Weight: _____   Exercise: _____   Battle Buddy: _____

Breakfast	Lunch	Dinner	Snacks
_____	_____	_____	_____
_____	_____	_____	_____
_____	_____	_____	_____
_____	_____	_____	**Water**
_____	_____	_____	_____

Today's Scripture: Philippians 3:12-14

Everyone has excuses for weight-loss failure. What are some of the circumstances or people you have blamed? _____

_____

_____

_____

_____

What does verse thirteen say you should do in regard to your past? _____

_____

_____

What can you do to put those excuses behind you? _____

_____

_____

New insights: _____

_____

_____

Prayer for today: _____

_____

_____

Victories/defeats today: _____

_____

_____

Week 5   *Saturday*   *Why You Fail*

Weight: _____   **Exercise:** _____   **Battle Buddy:** _____

Breakfast	Lunch	Dinner	Snacks
_____	_____	_____	_____
_____	_____	_____	_____
_____	_____	_____	**Water**
_____	_____	_____	
_____	_____	_____	_____

Today's Scripture: Romans 7:14-25

You will suffer defeats in life, but that does not mean you are a failure. You are a failure only if you quit trying. Defeats are positive because they reveal character flaws. What flaws have been revealed to you in the past four weeks? _____

_____

_____

_____

_____

_____

_____

_____

The Apostle Paul had ups and downs, but to whom did he look for ultimate victory? _____

Who or what are you looking to for victory? _____

_____

New insights: _____

_____

_____

Prayer for today: _____

_____

_____

_____

Victories/defeats today: _____

_____

_____

WEEK SIX

MOTIVES AND GOALS

Brethren, I do not count myself to have apprehended;
but one thing I do, forgetting those things which are behind
and reaching forward to those things which are ahead.
I press toward the goal for the prize of the
upward call of God in Christ Jesus.
Philippians 3:13-14

Week 6   *Motives and Goals*

Weekly memory verses: Philippians 3:13-14

Review chapter seven (*Motives and Goals*) in the book *Winning the Battle of the Bulge*.

Motives and goals are deeply intertwined, especially when it comes to weight loss. Perhaps the focus of your goal is an event such as a wedding, class or family reunion, or a job interview. You want to look good to impress someone, or perhaps you want to avoid embarrassment. But what will happen when the event has passed? What will then motivate you to keep the weight off?

Your thinking needs to be transformed to shift your focus from self to Christ. It is not *"What do others think about me?"*, but *"What does Christ think about me?"*. It is not *"Look how great I am for losing weight,"* but *"Look how great he is for giving me victory."*

As you obey and trust your commander in chief and get to know him better, you will love him more and want to please him.

Week 6   *Sunday, Day 1*   *Motives and Goals*

Date: _____ **Weight**: _____

Weekly Overview (food battles you will you encounter this week):
Battle: _____ Day: _____
Battle plan: _____

Battle: _____ Day: _____
Battle plan: _____

Battle: _____ Day: _____
Battle plan: _____

Battle: _____ Day: _____
Battle plan: _____

Goals: _____
_____
_____

Battle Buddy: _____ **Phone**: _____
E-mail: _____ **Prayer needs**: _____
_____
_____

Character quality: _____
Why you need to develop this: _____
_____
_____
_____

Prayer for the week: _____
_____
_____
_____
_____
_____

Week 6   *Monday*   *Motives and Goals*

Weight: _____   Exercise: _____   Battle Buddy: _____

Breakfast	Lunch	Dinner	Snacks
_____	_____	_____	_____
_____	_____	_____	_____
_____	_____	_____	
_____	_____	_____	**Water**
_____	_____	_____	_____

Today's Scripture: Colossians 3:22-24

Today is a day for *total* honesty. Write down every motive you have used for trying to lose weight in the past. _____
_____
_____
_____
_____
_____

Who are you to please in everything you do? _____

Circle the motives above that you feel are pleasing to God. Put an X by the motives that are purely self-centered.

What can you do to change your motives to be God-centered? _____
_____
_____
_____

New insights: _____
_____
_____

Prayer for today: _____
_____
_____
_____

Victories/defeats today: _____
_____
_____

Week 6   *Tuesday*   *Motives and Goals*

Weight: _____ Exercise: _____ Battle Buddy: _____

Breakfast	Lunch	Dinner	Snacks
_____	_____	_____	_____
_____	_____	_____	_____
_____	_____	_____	_____
_____	_____	_____	**Water**
_____	_____	_____	_____

Today's Scripture: 1 Peter 3:1-5

The primary application of these verses is to husbands and wives. However, read these verses now with your weight-loss motives and goals in mind. Is it wrong to want your outward appearance to be attractive? _____

_____

When does it become wrong? _____

_____

_____

_____

Do you put *too much* emphasis on outward appearance? _____

Do you put *enough* emphasis on outward appearance? _____ How will losing weight give you an inner beauty that can be seen by others? _____

_____

_____

_____

New insights: _____

_____

_____

Prayer for today: _____

_____

_____

_____

Victories/defeats today: _____

_____

_____

Week 6   *Wednesday*   *Motives and Goals*

Weight: _____   Exercise: _____   Battle Buddy: _____

Breakfast	Lunch	Dinner	Snacks
_____	_____	_____	_____
_____	_____	_____	_____
_____	_____	_____	**Water**
_____	_____	_____	
_____	_____	_____	

Today's Scripture: James 1:21-25

What does verse 22 say you are doing if you hear the Word but don't obey? _____

_____

Sometimes your motives will not be pure. How should you conduct yourself regardless of your motives? _____

_____

_____

_____

_____

Sometimes you tell yourself that if you don't have proper motives, you should give up. In what circumstances or at what times have you done this? _____

_____

_____

_____

_____

New insights: _____

_____

_____

Prayer for today: _____

_____

_____

_____

Victories/defeats today: _____

_____

_____

Week 6   ***Thursday***   *Motives and Goals*

Weight: _____   Exercise: _____   Battle Buddy: _____

Breakfast	Lunch	Dinner	Snacks
_____	_____	_____	_____
_____	_____	_____	_____
_____	_____	_____	**Water**
_____	_____	_____	
_____	_____	_____	_____

Today's Scripture: Matthew 6:25-34

How have you let food become more important than life? _____

_____

_____

_____

How have you rejected the healthy foods God wants to feed you? _____

_____

_____

How can you seek God's kingdom in your eating and exercise habits? _____

_____

_____

_____

What future things have you worried about regarding eating habits? _____

_____

_____

New insights: _____

_____

_____

Prayer for today: _____

_____

_____

Victories/defeats today: _____

_____

_____

Week 6   *Friday*   *Motives and Goals*

Weight: _____   **Exercise:** _____   **Battle Buddy:** _____

Breakfast	Lunch	Dinner	Snacks
_____	_____	_____	_____
_____	_____	_____	_____
_____	_____	_____	**Water**
_____	_____	_____	_____
_____	_____	_____	

Today's Scripture: Matthew 5:13-16

As a believer, you are to be the salt and light of the world. How can proper eating glorify the Father before the world? _____

_____

_____

_____

_____

_____

_____

_____

What will happen when the world sees your good deeds? _____

_____

_____

New insights: _____

_____

Prayer for today: _____

_____

_____

Victories/defeats today: _____

_____

_____

Week 6   *Saturday*   *Motives and Goals*

Weight: _____   Exercise: _____   Battle Buddy: _____

Breakfast	Lunch	Dinner	Snacks
_____	_____	_____	_____
_____	_____	_____	_____
_____	_____	_____	
_____	_____	_____	**Water**
_____	_____	_____	_____

Today's Scripture: 1 John 2:15-16

How have you shown a *love* of the world regarding overeating? _____

_____

_____

_____

Verse sixteen says that *greed, envy,* and *pride* do not come from the Father but from the world. Answer the first question again with each of these words in mind.

Greed: _____

_____

_____

Pride: _____

_____

_____

Envy: _____

_____

New insights: _____

_____

_____

Prayer for today: _____

_____

_____

Victories/defeats today: _____

_____

_____

KNOWING YOUR COMMANDER IN CHIEF

Yet I am not ashamed, because I know whom I have believed,
and am convinced that he is able to guard what
I have entrusted to him for that day.
2 Timothy 1:12b

Week 7   *Know Your Commander*

Weekly memory verse: 2 Timothy 1:12b

Review chapter eight (*Knowing Your Commander in Chief*) in the book *Winning the Battle of the Bulge*.

God's army is not one in which a soldier's rank rises over the years. Rather, the longer one is in God's army, and the more intimately the commander in chief is known, the soldier becomes more of a servant. *Your* rank becomes lower as you rank *him* higher.

You are not in charge; he is.
You do not give orders; you follow his.
You do not devise plans for your life; you follow his plans for you.
You do not deserve victory; he freely gives it.

God knows each battle, each defeat, each victory, and he knows the end from the beginning. He will pick you up when you fall and carry you when you cannot go on.

God is your shield, your protector, your defense, your high tower, and so much more, but only as long as you remain under his authority and protection through obedience.

Week 7   *Sunday, Day 1*   *Know Your Commander*

Date: _____ **Weight**: _____

Weekly Overview (food battles you will you encounter this week):
Battle: _____ Day: _____
Battle plan: _____

Battle: _____ Day: _____
Battle plan: _____

Battle: _____ Day: _____
Battle plan: _____

Battle: _____ Day: _____
Battle plan: _____

Goals: _____
_____
_____

Battle Buddy: _____ **Phone**: _____
E-mail: _____ **Prayer needs**: _____
_____
_____

Character quality:_____
Why you need to develop this: _____
_____
_____
_____

Prayer for the week: _____
_____
_____
_____
_____
_____
_____

Week 7   *Monday*   *Know Your Commander*

Weight: _____ Exercise: _____ Battle Buddy: _____

Breakfast	**Lunch**	**Dinner**	**Snacks**
_____	_____	_____	_____
_____	_____	_____	_____
_____	_____	_____	**Water**
_____	_____	_____	_____
_____	_____	_____	

Today's Scripture: Joshua 5:13-15

Who is the man who appeared to Joshua? _____
What is his title? _____

What two things did Joshua do when he realized to whom he was speaking?
1) _____
_____

2) _____
_____

What act(s) of obedience and worship can you do today that will show the Lord
he is your commander in chief? _____
_____
_____
_____
_____

New insights: _____
_____
_____

Prayer for today: _____
_____
_____
_____

Victories/defeats today: _____
_____
_____

Week 7   *Tuesday*   *Know Your Commander*

Weight: _____   Exercise: _____   Battle Buddy: _____

Breakfast	Lunch	Dinner	Snacks
_____	_____	_____	_____
_____	_____	_____	_____
_____	_____	_____	_____
_____	_____	_____	**Water**
_____	_____	_____	_____

Today's Scripture: Matthew 8:18-22

What excuses are you still using for not being completely obedient? _____

_____

_____

_____

_____

_____

_____

What steps will you take to put excuses behind you? _____

_____

_____

_____

_____

_____

_____

New insights: _____

_____

_____

Prayer for today: _____

_____

_____

Victories/defeats today: _____

_____

_____

Week 7   *Wednesday*   *Know Your Commander*

Weight: _____   **Exercise:** _____   **Battle Buddy:** _____

Breakfast	Lunch	Dinner	Snacks
_____	_____	_____	_____
_____	_____	_____	_____
_____	_____	_____	**Water**
_____	_____	_____	
_____	_____	_____	_____

Today's Scripture: 1 Corinthians 3:9-11

What is the foundation on which you are to build your life? _____
_____

What or who has been your foundation in the past regarding your battle of the bulge? _____
_____
_____
_____

What specific building materials can you use to make your battle of the bulge a success? _____
_____
_____
_____
_____
_____

New insights: _____
_____
_____

Prayer for today: _____
_____
_____
_____

Victories/defeats today: _____
_____
_____

Week 7   *Thursday*   *Know Your Commander*

Weight: _____   Exercise: _____   Battle Buddy: _____

Breakfast	Lunch	Dinner	Snacks
_____	_____	_____	_____
_____	_____	_____	_____
_____	_____	_____	**Water**
_____	_____	_____	
_____	_____	_____	

Today's Scripture: Philippians 2:5-8

Who should you think like? _____

How can you make thinking like Christ a reality in your life? _____

_____

_____

_____

What character quality did Jesus exhibit? _____

Jesus was obedient to the Father to the point of _____ .

How have you not been obedient to your commander in chief in your battle of the bulge? _____

_____

_____

_____

_____

New insights: _____

_____

_____

Prayer for today: _____

_____

_____

_____

Victories/defeats today: _____

_____

_____

Week 7 *Friday* *Know Your Commander*

Weight: _____ Exercise: _____ Battle Buddy: _____

Breakfast	**Lunch**	**Dinner**	**Snacks**
_____	_____	_____	_____
_____	_____	_____	_____
_____	_____	_____	_____
_____	_____	_____	**Water**
_____	_____	_____	_____

Today's Scripture: 1 Samuel 15:22-23

What does God delight in more than sacrifices? _____

List the "sacrifices" you made in the past when you were dieting. _____

_____

_____

_____

What was wrong with those sacrifices? _____

_____

_____

_____

On what specific areas of obedience do you need to work? _____

_____

_____

_____

New insights: _____

_____

_____

Prayer for today: _____

_____

_____

_____

Victories/defeats today: _____

_____

_____

Week 7   *Saturday*   *Know Your Commander*

Weight: _____   Exercise: _____   Battle Buddy: _____

Breakfast	Lunch	Dinner	Snacks
_____	_____	_____	_____
_____	_____	_____	_____
_____	_____	_____	**Water**
_____	_____	_____	
_____	_____	_____	_____

Today's Scripture: Psalm 46

What will God do for you when you are in trouble? _____

_____

_____

Why is there no need for you to be afraid? _____

_____

_____

Who is always with you? _____

How do you see your commander in chief differently than you did previously?

_____

_____

_____

_____

New insights: _____

_____

_____

Prayer for today: _____

_____

_____

_____

Victories/defeats today: _____

_____

_____

USING YOUR WEAPONS

*For though we live in the world, we do not wage war
as the world does. The weapons we fight with are not the weapons of
the world. On the contrary, they have divine power to
demolish strongholds. We demolish arguments and every pretension
that sets itself up against the knowledge of God,
and we take captive every thought to make it obedient to Christ.*
2 Corinthians 10:3-5

Week 8   *Weapons*

Weekly memory verses: 2 Corinthians 10:3-5

Review chapters nine (*Using Your Weapons*) and thirteen (*Support From the Home Front*) in the book *Winning the Battle of the Bulge*.

The Scriptures tell you to be ready with your spiritual armor and weapons. Sometimes you are to be on the defensive, and other times you are to be aggressively offensive; there are even times when you are to flee.

Your battle of the bulge is not fought against a traditional enemy; therefore, you will not fight with traditional weapons. Because the enemy attacks you physically, mentally and emotionally, and spiritually, your battles will be fought in those areas.

As you read this week's Scripture verses, consider how you can apply each verse to yourself in those three areas. Ask God to show you which weapons to use in your unique circumstances. Use the columns below to list the weapons you might use to fight your battle.

Physically	*Mentally/Emotionally*	*Spiritually*

Week 8   *Sunday, Day 1*   *Weapons*

Date: _____ **Weight**: _____

Weekly Overview (food battles you will you encounter this week):
Battle: _____ Day: _____
Battle plan: _____

Battle: _____ Day: _____
Battle plan: _____

Battle: _____ Day: _____
Battle plan: _____

Battle: _____ Day: _____
Battle plan: _____

Goals: _____
_____
_____

Battle Buddy: _____ **Phone**: _____
E-mail: _____ **Prayer needs**: _____
_____
_____

Character quality: _____
Why you need to develop this: _____
_____
_____
_____

Prayer for the week: _____
_____
_____
_____
_____
_____
_____

Week 8   *Monday*   *Weapons*

Weight: _____   **Exercise:** _____   **Battle Buddy:** _____

Breakfast	Lunch	Dinner	Snacks
_____	_____	_____	_____
_____	_____	_____	_____
_____	_____	_____	**Water**
_____	_____	_____	_____
_____	_____	_____	

Today's Scripture: Ephesians 6:10-17

How much of God's armor do you need to put on? _____

In whose power and might do you fight? _____

What will God's armor do for you? _____

_____

_____

_____

_____

Why is it vital that you fight in God's strength and power? _____

_____

_____

_____

New insights: _____

_____

Prayer for today: _____

_____

_____

Victories/defeats today: _____

_____

_____

Week 8   *Tuesday*   *Weapons*

Weight: _____ Exercise: _____ Battle Buddy: _____

Breakfast	Lunch	Dinner	Snacks
_____	_____	_____	_____
_____	_____	_____	_____
_____	_____	_____	_____
_____	_____	_____	**Water**
_____	_____	_____	_____

Today's Scripture: Repeat Ephesians 6:10-17

Apply each weapon or piece of armor to your battle.

Belt of Truth _____

_____

Breastplate of Righteousness _____

_____

Gospel of Peace _____

_____

Shield of Faith _____

_____

Helmet of Salvation _____

_____

Sword of the Spirit (Word of God) _____

_____

New insights: _____

_____

_____

Prayer for today: _____

_____

_____

Victories/defeats today: _____

_____

_____

Week 8   *Wednesday*   *Weapons*

Weight: _____   **Exercise:** _____   **Battle Buddy:** _____

Breakfast	Lunch	Dinner	Snacks
_____	_____	_____	_____
_____	_____	_____	_____
_____	_____	_____	**Water**
_____	_____	_____	
_____	_____	_____	

Today's Scripture: Ephesians 6:18

What additional weapon do you have to fight the enemy? _____
_____

What can you do to make prayer a more effective weapon? _____
_____
_____
_____
_____

List any changes you need to make in your personal prayer time. _____
_____
_____
_____
_____
_____
_____

New insights: _____
_____
_____

Prayer for today: _____
_____
_____
_____

Victories/defeats today: _____
_____
_____

Week 8   *Thursday*   *Weapons*

Weight: _____ **Exercise:** _____ **Battle Buddy:** _____

Breakfast	Lunch	Dinner	Snacks
_____	_____	_____	_____
_____	_____	_____	_____
_____	_____	_____	**Water**
_____	_____	_____	_____

Today's Scripture: Romans 13:11-14

What works of darkness do you need to cast off in your battle of the bulge? _____

_____

_____

_____

_____

_____

What are you to put on in place of works of darkness? _____

_____

In what areas do you make provision for self-indulgence? _____

_____

_____

_____

_____

_____

New insights: _____

_____

_____

Prayer for today: _____

_____

_____

_____

Victories/defeats today: _____

_____

_____

Week 8   *Friday*   *Weapons*

Weight: _____   Exercise: _____   Battle Buddy: _____

Breakfast	Lunch	Dinner	Snacks
_____	_____	_____	_____
_____	_____	_____	_____
_____	_____	_____	**Water**
_____	_____	_____	
_____	_____	_____	_____

Today's Scripture: 2 Corinthians 10:3-5

What is unique about the weapons Christians use in battle? _____
_____
_____
_____

What kind of power do your weapons have? _____
_____

What can your divine weapons do when you put them to use? _____
_____
_____
_____
_____
_____
_____

New insights: _____
_____
_____

Prayer for today: _____
_____
_____
_____

Victories/defeats today: _____
_____
_____

Week 8   *Saturday*   *Weapons*

Weight: _____   **Exercise:** _____   **Battle Buddy:** _____

Breakfast	Lunch	Dinner	Snacks
_____	_____	_____	_____
_____	_____	_____	_____
_____	_____	_____	**Water**
_____	_____	_____	
_____	_____	_____	_____

Today's Scripture: Hebrews 4:12-13

The Word of God is _____ and _____ .

The Word of God judges the _____ and _____

_____ .

Have you tried to hide any of your eating habits from God? _____

_____

_____

_____

_____

_____

_____

_____

_____

_____

New insights: _____

_____

_____

Prayer for today: _____

_____

_____

_____

Victories/defeats today: _____

_____

_____

DEVELOPING GODLY CHARACTER

I beseech you therefore, brethren, by the mercies of God, that you present your bodies a living sacrifice, holy, acceptable to God, which is your reasonable service. And do not be conformed to this world, but be transformed by the renewing of your mind, that you may prove what is that good and acceptable and perfect will of God.
Romans 12:1-2

Week 9   *Developing Godly Character*

Weekly memory verse: Romans 12:1-2

Review chapter ten (*Developing Godly Character*) in the book *Winning the Battle of the Bulge*.

Everyone has positive character qualities and negative character qualities. Depending on a person's personality and temperament, some of these qualities tend to come more naturally than others. You should strive to develop positive godly character qualities throughout your life even when they do not come easily or naturally.

It is possible to have developed strong character in one area and to lack character in another area. For instance, you may have great self-control when it comes to what and how much television you watch, but have little self-control when it comes to what and how much food you eat.

Boot camp is a time when soldiers strengthen existing character and learn additional character. You are now beyond "boot camp", but you will spend the rest of your life strengthening the character you already have and allowing God to develop more in you.

This week you will look at twenty-five character qualities. Write down what you think each one means and then apply each one to your battle of the bulge. Note which ones need more work and those at which you have already achieved some success. The list is not inclusive; feel free to add other character qualities you might apply to your life.

Week 9   *Sunday, 1*   *Character*

Date: _____ **Weight**: _____

Weekly Overview (food battles you will you encounter this week):
Battle: _____ Day: _____
Battle plan: _____

Battle: _____ Day: _____
Battle plan: _____

Battle: _____ Day: _____
Battle plan: _____

Battle: _____ Day: _____
Battle plan: _____

Goals: _____
_____
_____

Battle Buddy: _____ **Phone**: _____
E-mail: _____ **Prayer needs**: _____
_____
_____

Character quality:_____
Why you need to develop this: _____
_____
_____
_____

Prayer for the week: _____
_____
_____
_____
_____
_____
_____

Week 9   *Monday*   *Character*

Weight: _____   **Exercise:** _____   **Battle Buddy:** _____

Breakfast	Lunch	Dinner	Snacks
_____	_____	_____	_____
_____	_____	_____	_____
_____	_____	_____	_____
_____	_____	_____	**Water**
_____	_____	_____	_____

Today's Scripture: Galatians 5:16-26

Focus: _____
_____
_____

Contentment: _____
_____
_____
_____

Joyfulness: _____
_____
_____

Perseverance: _____
_____
_____

New insights: _____
_____
_____

Prayer for today: _____
_____
_____
_____

Victories/defeats today: _____
_____
_____

Week 9   *Tuesday*   *Character*

Weight: _____   **Exercise:** _____   **Battle Buddy:** _____

Breakfast	Lunch	Dinner	Snacks
_____	_____	_____	_____
_____	_____	_____	_____
_____	_____	_____	**Water**
_____	_____	_____	_____
_____	_____	_____	

Today's Scripture: 2 Peter 1:2-8

Diligence: _____
_____
_____

Patience: _____
_____
_____
_____

Self-Control: _____
_____
_____

Integrity: _____
_____
_____

New insights: _____
_____
_____

Prayer for today: _____
_____
_____
_____

Victories/defeats today: _____
_____
_____

Week 9   *Wednesday*   *Character*

Weight: _____   **Exercise:** _____   **Battle Buddy:** _____

Breakfast	Lunch	Dinner	Snacks
_____	_____	_____	_____
_____	_____	_____	_____
_____	_____	_____	**Water**
_____	_____	_____	_____

Today's Scripture: Colossians 2:1-8

Faithfulness: _____
_____
_____

Honesty: _____
_____
_____
_____

Courage: _____
_____
_____
_____

Vigilance: _____
_____
_____

New insights: _____
_____
_____

Prayer for today: _____
_____
_____
_____

Victories/defeats today: _____
_____
_____

Week 9   *Thursday*   *Character*

Weight: _____   **Exercise**: _____   **Battle Buddy**: _____

Breakfast	Lunch	Dinner	Snacks
_____	_____	_____	_____
_____	_____	_____	_____
_____	_____	_____	**Water**
_____	_____	_____	
_____	_____	_____	_____

Today's Scripture: Colossians 1:19-23

Humility: _____

_____

_____

Responsibility: _____

_____

_____

_____

Honor: _____

_____

_____

_____

Accountability: _____

_____

_____

New insights: _____

_____

_____

Prayer for today: _____

_____

_____

Victories/defeats today: _____

_____

_____

Week 9   *Friday*   *Character*

Weight: _____   Exercise: _____   Battle Buddy: _____

Breakfast	Lunch	Dinner	Snacks
_____	_____	_____	_____
_____	_____	_____	_____
_____	_____	_____	**Water**
_____	_____	_____	_____
_____	_____	_____	

Today's Scripture: Ephesians 5:15-17

Exhortation: _____
_____
_____

Love: _____
_____
_____

Discernment: _____
_____
_____
_____

Decisiveness: _____
_____
_____

New insights: _____
_____
_____

Prayer for today: _____
_____
_____
_____

Victories/defeats today: _____
_____
_____

Week 9   *Saturday*   *Character*

Weight: _____   **Exercise**: _____   **Battle Buddy**: _____

Breakfast	Lunch	Dinner	Snacks
_____	_____	_____	_____
_____	_____	_____	_____
_____	_____	_____	**Water**
_____	_____	_____	
_____	_____	_____	_____

Today's Scripture: Ephesians 4:11-16

Discipline: _____
_____
_____

Loyalty: _____
_____
_____

Obedience: _____
_____
_____

Orderliness: _____
_____

Wisdom: _____
_____

New insights: _____
_____
_____

Prayer for today: _____
_____
_____
_____

Victories/defeats today: _____
_____
_____

GIVING GOD THE GLORY

So whether you eat or drink or whatever you do,
do it all for the glory of God.
1 Corinthians 10:31

For it is time for judgment to begin with the family of God.
1 Peter 4:17

Week 10   *Giving God the Glory*

Weekly memory verses: 1 Corinthians 10:31 and 1 Peter 4:17

Review chapters eleven (*Giving God the Glory*) and fourteen (*Commanding Officers: Practicing What You Preach*) in the book *Winning the Battle of the Bulge*.

Your purpose in life is to glorify Christ. He is glorified when your life is transformed to be more like him, when you think like him, act like him, treat others as he would treat them, give as he would give, pray as he would pray, worship as he would worship, and yes, even take care of your body as he took care of his earthly body.

If your goal is to lose weight and feel good about yourself (giving *yourself* the glory), you may or may not do it. If your goal is to glorify *God* by transforming your thinking and your actions to be more like Christ and to obediently submit every area of your life to his authority, you *will* lose weight.

Do you understand that the concept of this book is not about losing weight, but rather about glorifying God with every part of your being; it is about learning what submission and obedience are; it is about standing alongside your commander in chief as he defeats the enemy?

Week 10   *Sunday, Day 1*   *Giving God the Glory*

Date: _____ **Weight**: _____

Weekly Overview (food battles you will you encounter this week):
Battle: _____ Day: _____
Battle plan: _____

Battle: _____ Day: _____
Battle plan: _____

Battle: _____ Day: _____
Battle plan: _____

Battle: _____ Day: _____
Battle plan: _____

Goals:_____
_____
_____

Battle Buddy: _____ **Phone**: _____
E-mail: _____ **Prayer needs**: _____
_____
_____

Character quality:_____
Why you need to develop this: _____
_____
_____
_____

Prayer for the week: _____
_____
_____
_____
_____
_____
_____

Week 10   *Monday*   *Giving God the Glory*

Weight: _____   **Exercise:** _____   **Battle Buddy:** _____

Breakfast	Lunch	Dinner	Snacks
_____	_____	_____	_____
_____	_____	_____	_____
_____	_____	_____	**Water**
_____	_____	_____	_____
_____	_____	_____	

Today's Scripture: 2 Corinthians 3:17-18

What will you experience when you allow the Spirit of God to work in your life?

What new freedoms have you experienced in the past ten weeks? _____
_____
_____
_____

What should your life reflect? _____
_____

In what areas do you feel God is transforming your life? Be specific. _____
_____
_____
_____
_____

New insights: _____
_____
_____

Prayer for today: _____
_____
_____
_____

Victories/defeats today: _____
_____
_____

Week 10   *Tuesday*   *Giving God the Glory*

Weight: _____ Exercise: _____ Battle Buddy: _____

Breakfast	**Lunch**	**Dinner**	**Snacks**
_____	_____	_____	_____
_____	_____	_____	_____
_____	_____	_____	_____
_____	_____	_____	**Water**
_____	_____	_____	_____

Today's Scripture: 2 Corinthians 4:7-11

From where does your power come? _____

_____

What should your attitude be in the midst of discouragements and trials? _____

_____
_____
_____
_____
_____
_____
_____
_____

Whose life is to be to manifested in your body? _____

_____

New insights: _____

_____
_____

Prayer for today: _____

_____
_____
_____

Victories/defeats today: _____

_____
_____

Week 10   *Wednesday*   *Giving God the Glory*

Weight: _____   Exercise: _____   Battle Buddy: _____

Breakfast	Lunch	Dinner	Snacks
_____	_____	_____	_____
_____	_____	_____	_____
_____	_____	_____	**Water**
_____	_____	_____	_____

Today's Scripture: 2 Corinthians 6:14–7:1

Your body is the temple of the Holy Spirit.

From what foods do you need to *refrain*? _____
_____
_____
_____

What foods do you need to *limit*? _____
_____
_____

Are there circumstances or people in your life who hinder your relationship with Christ? _____
_____
_____
_____

New insights: _____
_____
_____

Prayer for today: _____
_____
_____
_____

Victories/defeats today: _____
_____
_____

Week 10   *Thursday*   *Giving God the Glory*

Weight: _____   Exercise: _____   Battle Buddy: _____

Breakfast	Lunch	Dinner	Snacks
_____	_____	_____	_____
_____	_____	_____	_____
_____	_____	_____	_____
_____	_____	_____	**Water**
_____	_____	_____	_____

Today's Scripture: Colossians 1:16

In what ways do you think you were personally created to give God glory? Be specific._____

_____

_____

_____

_____

_____

_____

_____

_____

_____

_____

_____

New insights: _____

_____

_____

Prayer for today: _____

_____

_____

Victories/defeats today: _____

_____

_____

Week 10   *Friday*   *Giving God the Glory*

Weight: _____   Exercise: _____   Battle Buddy: _____

Breakfast	Lunch	Dinner	Snacks
_____	_____	_____	_____
_____	_____	_____	_____
_____	_____	_____	_____
_____	_____	_____	**Water**
_____	_____	_____	_____

Today's Scripture: 1 Corinthians 6:12-20

To whom does your body belong? _____

Who lives within you? _____

Why is it important to keep your body sexually pure? _____
_____
_____
_____
_____
_____

Why is it important to keep your body nutritionally pure? _____
_____
_____
_____
_____

New insights: _____
_____
_____

Prayer for today: _____
_____
_____
_____

Victories/defeats today: _____
_____
_____

Week 10   *Saturday*   *Giving God the Glory*

Weight: _____ Exercise: _____ Battle Buddy: _____

Breakfast	Lunch	Dinner	Snacks
_____	_____	_____	_____
_____	_____	_____	_____
_____	_____	_____	**Water**
_____	_____	_____	_____

Today's Scripture: 1 Corinthians 10:31

How can what you eat give God glory? Be specific. _____

_____

_____

_____

_____

_____

How can what you eat rob God of glory? Be specific. _____

_____

_____

_____

_____

_____

New insights: _____

_____

_____

Prayer for today: _____

_____

_____

_____

Victories/defeats today: _____

_____

_____

WEEK ELEVEN

LOOKING YOUR BEST
FROM THE INSIDE OUT

*For you created my inmost being, you knit me together in my
mother's womb. I praise you because I am fearfully and wonderfully
made; your works are wonderful, I know that full well. My frame
was not hidden from you when I was made in the secret place.
When I was woven together in the depths of the earth, your eyes saw
my unformed body. All the days ordained for me were written in
your book before one of them came to be.*
Psalm 139:13-16

Week 11   *Outward Appearance*

Weekly memory verse*: Psalm 139:13-16

Review chapter twelve (*Looking Your Best from the Inside Out*) in the book
Winning the Battle of the Bulge.

It is sometimes difficult to find a balance between outward appearance and
inward beauty because everyone has a different concept and standard of how a
Christian should look and act. We know God cares about beauty because he is
the creator of all things beautiful. God says in 1 Samuel 16:7 "that man looks on
the outward appearance, but the Lord looks at the heart," yet five verses later, he
makes note of David's handsome features. Sarah, Rebekah, Rachel, Bathsheba, and
others are noted in Scripture as exceptional beauties.

We all make judgments based on outward appearance—people who are fat, thin,
or tattooed; girls in short skirts, tight blouses, heavy makeup, or no makeup; guys
in rumpled or dirty clothing. The list goes on and on.

Here are some guidelines on which I think we can all agree:
Our outward appearance should glorify Christ.
We have one opportunity to make a first impression.
*Our appearance (clothing, hair, makeup) should never be a distraction to our
Christian testimony.*
We should be modest in our attire.
We should be clean, neat, and devoid of body odor.

Read the Scripture each day and write your thoughts and insights into your personal
appearance and note any changes you think God wants to make in your life.

Week 11   *Sunday, Day 1*   *Outward Appearance*

Date: _____ **Weight:** _____

Weekly Overview (food battles you will you encounter this week):
Battle: _____ Day: _____
Battle plan: _____

Battle: _____ Day: _____
Battle plan: _____

Battle: _____ Day: _____
Battle plan: _____

Battle: _____ Day: _____
Battle plan: _____

Goals: _____
_____
_____

Battle Buddy: _____ **Phone:** _____
E-mail: _____ **Prayer needs:** _____
_____
_____

Character quality: _____
Why you need to develop this: _____
_____
_____
_____

Prayer for the week: _____
_____
_____
_____
_____
_____
_____

Week 11   *Monday*   *Outward Appearance*

Weight: _____ Exercise: _____ **Battle Buddy:** _____

Breakfast	Lunch	Dinner	Snacks
_____	_____	_____	_____
_____	_____	_____	_____
_____	_____	_____	**Water**
_____	_____	_____	_____

Today's Scripture: Genesis 24:1-22

How did Rebekah exhibit a balance of outward and inward beauty? _____

_____

_____

_____

_____

_____

How does your life exhibit a balance between outward and inward beauty? _____

_____

_____

_____

_____

_____

New insights: _____

_____

Prayer for today: _____

_____

_____

Victories/defeats today: _____

_____

_____

Week 11   *Tuesday*   *Outward Appearance*

Weight: _____   Exercise: _____   Battle Buddy: _____

Breakfast	Lunch	Dinner	Snacks
_____	_____	_____	_____
_____	_____	_____	_____
_____	_____	_____	**Water**
_____	_____	_____	
_____		_____	_____

Today's Scripture: Isaiah 64:8

God has formed you and chosen you for his service. As a believer in Christ, you belong to him. Are you pliable clay in his hands, or are you hardened and bitter?

In what ways do you resist allowing God to mold you?

Physically _____

_____

Mentally/Emotionally _____

_____

Spiritually _____

_____

_____

New insights: _____

_____

Prayer for today: _____

_____

_____

Victories/defeats today: _____

_____

_____

Week 11   *Wednesday*   *Outward Appearance*

Weight: _____   **Exercise**: _____   **Battle Buddy**: _____

Breakfast	**Lunch**	**Dinner**	**Snacks**
_____	_____	_____	_____
_____	_____	_____	_____
_____	_____	_____	_____
_____	_____	_____	**Water**
_____	_____	_____	_____

Today's Scripture: 2 Corinthians 10:12, 17-18

In what ways have you compared yourself with others?

Physically _____ _____
_____
_____

Mentally/Emotionally _____
_____
_____

Spiritually _____
_____
_____

Why is it unwise to compare yourself with others? _____
_____
_____

New insights: _____
_____
_____

Prayer for today: _____
_____
_____
_____

Victories/defeats today: _____
_____
_____

Week 11　　　　　*Thursday*　　　*Outward Appearance*

Weight: _____　Exercise: _____　Battle Buddy: _____

Breakfast	Lunch	Dinner	Snacks
_____	_____	_____	_____
_____	_____	_____	_____
_____	_____	_____	**Water**
_____	_____	_____	_____
_____	_____	_____	

Today's Scripture: 1 Samuel 16:1-13

In verse seven, God told Samuel to look at the _____ heart, not
just the _____ appearance. Yet in verse twelve, David's handsome
features are noted. The inner attitude of your heart is of utmost importance and
will reflect outwardly toward other people. But God also created outward beauty.
Why are both important? _____

_____

_____

_____

_____

_____

_____

_____

_____

New insights: _____

_____

Prayer for today: _____

_____

_____

Victories/defeats today: _____

_____

_____

Week 11   *Friday*   *Outward Appearance*

Weight: _____ Exercise: _____ Battle Buddy: _____

Breakfast	Lunch	Dinner	Snacks
_____	_____	_____	_____
_____	_____	_____	_____
_____	_____	_____	Water
_____	_____	_____	_____
_____	_____	_____	

Today's Scripture: 1 Timothy 4:12

How might your *actions* and *appearance* be an example to others in:

Speech _____

_____

Attitude _____

_____

Love _____

_____

_____

Faith _____

_____

Modesty _____

_____

New insights: _____

_____

_____

Prayer for today: _____

_____

_____

Victories/defeats today: _____

_____

_____

Week 11   *Saturday*   *Outward Appearance*

Weight: _____   Exercise: _____   Battle Buddy: _____

Breakfast	Lunch	Dinner	Snacks
_____	_____	_____	_____
_____	_____	_____	_____
_____	_____	_____	**Water**
_____	_____	_____	
_____	_____	_____	_____

Today's Scripture: Psalm 139:13-16

Verse fourteen says you are _____ and ____
_____ made. When did God plan your body?

Do you completely accept the way God made you? _____

If not, what *unchangeable* physical features do you need to accept as a gift from God? _____
_____
_____

How can you use those features to glorify Christ? _____
_____
_____
_____
_____

New insights: _____
_____
_____

Prayer for today: _____
_____
_____
_____

Victories/defeats today: _____
_____
_____

WEEK TWELVE

BATTLING FOR LIFE

Therefore, since we are surrounded by such a great
cloud of witnesses, let us throw off everything that hinders
and the sin that so easily entangles,
and let us run with perseverance the race marked out for us.
Let us fix our eyes on Jesus, the author and perfecter of our faith,
who for the joy set before him endured the cross, scorning its shame,
and sat down at the right hand of the throne of God.
Hebrews 12:1-2

Week 12   *Battling for Life*

Weekly memory verses: Hebrews 12:1-2

Review chapter sixteen (*Battling for Life: Victorious for Eternity*) in the book *Winning the Battle of the Bulge*.

You have spent twelve weeks planning and preparing for your battle of the bulge. You have: enlisted in the Lord's Army, been through boot camp, discovered why you have failed in the past, redirected your motives, learned about your enemy and commander in chief, and learned which weapons to use in warfare. You have let the Lord speak to you through his Word, and you have told him the deepest secrets and longings of your heart. It is my prayer that you truly understand that your battle of the bulge is about obedience to the Lord, building godly character into your life, and glorifying him in everything you do. *Winning the battle of the bulge is **not** just about the weight!*

Until now, you have been fighting daily battles in your war, but today you are signing up for a life of service and obedience in God's army; today is the first day of the rest of your military career. There is no retirement in this war, not until you reach your heavenly home with Christ. He *is* and has provided your ultimate victory.

As you read the Scriptures, pray, and journal this week, ask God to be with you as commit your life to him anew.

Week 12   *Sunday, Day 1*   *Battling for Life*

Date: _____ **Weight**: _____

Weekly Overview (food battles you will you encounter this week):
Battle: _____ Day: _____
Battle plan: _____

Battle: _____ Day: _____
Battle plan: _____

Battle: _____ Day: _____
Battle plan: _____

Battle: _____ Day: _____
Battle plan: _____

Goals: _____
_____
_____

Battle Buddy: _____ **Phone**: _____
E-mail: _____ **Prayer needs**: _____
_____
_____

Character quality: _____
Why you need to develop this: _____
_____
_____
_____

Prayer for the week: _____
_____
_____
_____
_____
_____
_____

Week 12   *Monday*   *Battling for Life*

Weight: _____   Exercise: _____   Battle Buddy: _____

Breakfast	Lunch	Dinner	Snacks
_____	_____	_____	_____
_____	_____	_____	_____
_____	_____	_____	
_____	_____	_____	**Water**
_____	_____	_____	_____

Today's Scripture: Galatians 4:8-9

List any pitfalls that may cause you to go back to your former habits. Be specific.

_____

_____

_____

_____

_____

_____

Is anything still enslaving you? _____

_____

_____

_____

_____

_____

_____

New insights: _____

_____

_____

Prayer for today: _____

_____

_____

_____

Victories/defeats today: _____

_____

_____

Week 12   *Tuesday*   *Battling for Life*

Weight: _____   **Exercise:** _____   **Battle Buddy:** _____

Breakfast	**Lunch**	**Dinner**	**Snacks**
_____	_____	_____	_____
_____	_____	_____	_____
_____	_____	_____	_____
_____	_____	_____	**Water**
_____	_____	_____	_____

Today's Scripture: Psalm 84

How are you resting and dwelling with the Lord differently than you did twelve weeks ago? Be specific. _____

_____

_____

_____

_____

_____

_____

_____

_____

_____

_____

_____

_____

_____

New insights: _____

_____

_____

Prayer for today: _____

_____

_____

_____

Victories/defeats today: _____

_____

_____

Week 12   *Wednesday*   *Battling for Life*

Weight: _____   **Exercise:** _____   **Battle Buddy:** _____

Breakfast	Lunch	Dinner	Snacks
_____	_____	_____	_____
_____	_____	_____	_____
_____	_____	_____	**Water**
_____	_____	_____	
_____	_____	_____	_____

Today's Scripture: Galatians 5:1

List the reasons why you do not want to go back to your former way of eating and dieting. Be specific. _____

_____

_____

_____

_____

_____

_____

_____

_____

_____

_____

_____

_____

New insights: _____

_____

_____

Prayer for today: _____

_____

_____

_____

Victories/defeats today: _____

_____

_____

Week 12   *Thursday*   *Battling for Life*

Weight: _____   Exercise: _____   Battle Buddy: _____

Breakfast	Lunch	Dinner	Snacks
_____	_____	_____	_____
_____	_____	_____	_____
_____	_____	_____	_____
_____	_____	_____	**Water**
_____	_____	_____	_____

Today's Scripture: Galatians 6:6-10

What negative consequences have you reaped from improper eating? _____
_____
_____
_____
_____

What positive results have you reaped from your new lifestyle? _____
_____
_____
_____
_____

What are you going to do when you are battle weary and feel like giving up? ____
_____
_____
_____

New insights: _____
_____
_____

Prayer for today: _____
_____
_____

Victories/defeats today: _____
_____
_____

Week 12   *Friday*   *Battling for Life*

Weight: _____   Exercise: _____   Battle Buddy: _____

Breakfast	Lunch	Dinner	Snacks
_____	_____	_____	_____
_____	_____	_____	_____
_____	_____	_____	**Water**
_____	_____	_____	_____
_____	_____	_____	

Today's Scripture: Romans 5:1-5

How does a person experience peace with God? _____
_____

What should your attitude be when you encounter trials? _____
_____

Suffering will produce _____
Perseverance will produce _____
Character will produce _____

How will each of these help you maintain your commitment of obedience to the Lord? _____
_____
_____
_____
_____

New insights: _____
_____
_____

Prayer for today: _____
_____
_____
_____

Victories/defeats today: _____
_____
_____

Week 12   *Saturday*   *Battling for Life*

Weight: _____   Exercise: _____   Battle Buddy: _____

Breakfast	Lunch	Dinner	Snacks
_____	_____	_____	_____
_____	_____	_____	_____
_____	_____	_____	_____
_____	_____	_____	**Water**
_____	_____	_____	_____

Today's Scripture: 1 John 1:5-10

Why is it important for you to continue to be truthful with God and yourself?

_____

_____

_____

When you sin, what should you do about it? _____

_____

_____

_____

_____

Are you deceiving yourself in any way about your eating habits? _____

_____

_____

_____

_____

New insights: _____

_____

_____

Prayer for today: _____

_____

_____

_____

Victories/defeats today: _____

_____

_____

VICTORIOUS FOR ETERNITY

If you are a lifelong dieter like me, you realize that the fight has just begun. You did not develop a weight problem overnight, and you will not solve the problem in just thirteen weeks. As you continue to search God's Word, you will discover new insights and help for your battle.

This workbook/journal is designed to help you through an entire year. The next two pages are provided for you as a master to make copies for weeks thirteen through fifty-two. You may keep the copies in a binder, or use a notebook with blank pages to create your own workbook/journal. Daily Scripture references are provided for the next forty weeks. Continue to begin each week on Sunday by planning and preparing for upcoming battles, and then write your thoughts and insights into the Scriptures you read each day.

Refer back to the book *Winning the Battle of the Bulge* for suggestions and encouragement as you keep on in your battle. Continue to take your measurements, weigh yourself on a regular basis, be accountable to your battle buddy, and keep track of the food you eat. You should also continue your Scripture memorization by choosing a verse from each week's list.

God bless you, and may you find victory in Christ,

Mary Englund Murphy

Date: _____ **Weight**: _____

Weekly Overview (food battles you will you encounter this week):
Battle: _____ Day: _____
Battle plan: _____

Battle: _____ Day: _____
Battle plan: _____

Battle: _____ Day: _____
Battle plan: _____

Battle: _____ Day: _____
Battle plan: _____

Goals:_____
_____
_____

Battle Buddy: _____ **Phone**: _____
E-mail: _____ **Prayer needs**: _____
_____
_____

Character quality:_____
Why you need to develop this: _____
_____
_____
_____

Prayer for the week: _____
_____
_____
_____
_____
_____
_____

Week _____   *Day*_____

Weight: _____   Exercise: _____   Battle Buddy: _____

Breakfast	Lunch	Dinner	Snacks
_____	_____	_____	_____
_____	_____	_____	_____
_____	_____	_____	_____
_____	_____	_____	**Water**
_____	_____	_____	_____

Today's Scripture:

_____
_____
_____
_____
_____
_____
_____
_____
_____
_____
_____
_____
_____
_____
_____
_____

New insights: _____
_____
_____

Prayer for today: _____
_____
_____

Victories/defeats today: _____
_____
_____

Week 13

Monday	Psalm 91:1-8
Tuesday	Psalm 91:9-16
Wednesday	Ephesians 2:19-22
Thursday	Ephesians 3:14-21
Friday	Philippians 2:1-5
Saturday	Colossians 3:1-10

Week 14

Monday	Proverbs 27:19
Tuesday	Psalm 62:5-8
Wednesday	Psalm 103:1-5
Thursday	Jeremiah 17:9-10
Friday	Philippians 1:9-11
Saturday	Psalm 140:6-7

Week 15

Monday	ebrews 3:12-15
Tuesday	2 Corinthians 4:16-18
Wednesday	2 Corinthians 5:20
Thursday	Romans 4:18-21
Friday	Ephesians 4:20-24
Saturday	Psalm 56: 3-4, 9-13

Week 16

Monday	2 Corinthian 5:9-10
Tuesday	1 Peter 3:15-16
Wednesday	Psalm 59:16-17
Thursday	Ecclesiastes 9:16-18
Friday	Proverbs 16:25
Saturday	Psalm 63:1-8

Week 17

Monday	Romans 8:1-11
Tuesday	Psalm 15
Wednesday	Matthew 7:7-8
Thursday	Psalm 141:1-4
Friday	Proverbs 24:10
Saturday	Psalm 68:1-3

Week 18

Monday	Isaiah 40:28-31
Tuesday	2 Corinthians 3:3-6
Wednesday	Proverbs 18:10
Thursday	Psalm 37:23-28
Friday	Psalm 69:1-3
Saturday	Psalm 69:13-18

Week 19

Monday	Psalm 9:9-10
Tuesday	Galatians 1:3-5
Wednesday	Matthew 11:28-30
Thursday	Ephesians 4:1-6
Friday	Psalm 1
Saturday	Colossians 3:12-17

Week 20

Monday	Proverbs 4:5-15
Tuesday	Ephesians 4:27
Wednesday	Psalm 18:1-6
Thursday	Psalm 94:17-19
Friday	Philippians 1:19-21
Saturday	Psalm 86:8-13

Week 21

Monday	Hebrews 6:10-12
Tuesday	Proverbs 1:1-7
Wednesday	Psalm 107:22-31
Thursday	Luke 12:34
Friday	Ephesians 5:8-10
Saturday	Psalm 73:21-28

Week 22

Monday	Isaiah 41:10
Tuesday	Deuteronomy 6:4-9
Wednesday	Psalm 105:1-5
Thursday	James 4:13-17
Friday	Proverbs 2:1-15
Saturday	Psalm 119:169-176

Week 23

Monday	2 John 4-6
Tuesday	Psalm 143:1-6
Wednesday	Matthew 20:1-16
Thursday	Psalm 86:14-17
Friday	Titus 2:7-8
Saturday	Psalm 86:1-7

Week 24

Monday	1 Timothy 1:18-20
Tuesday	Philippians 2:14-16
Wednesday	Psalm 36:5-11
Thursday	Isaiah 55:8-12
Friday	Mark 4:3-8, 13-20
Saturday	Luke 6:46-49

Week 25

Monday	2 Corinthians 2:14-17
Tuesday	1 Peter 3:8-12
Wednesday	Psalm 139:1-4
Thursday	Psalm 139:5-8
Friday	Psalm 139:9-12
Saturday	2 Corinthians 1:3-7

Week 26

Monday	Galatians 1:10
Tuesday	Ephesians 1:15-21
Wednesday	Psalm 16
Thursday	1 Thessalonians 1:2-3
Friday	Proverbs 3:13-26
Saturday	2 Corinthians 11:14

Week 27

Monday	Habakkuk 3:17-19
Tuesday	Psalm 62:1-2
Wednesday	Mark 12:29-30
Thursday	Romans 14:1-13
Friday	2 Corinthians 5:1-6
Saturday	Psalm 139:17-20

Week 28

Monday	Galatians 3:1-5
Tuesday	3 John 2-4, 11
Wednesday	2 Peter 1:16-21
Thursday	Isaiah 29:15-16
Friday	Psalm 119: 97-104
Saturday	Colossians 2:15

Week 29

Monday	Psalm 145:14-16
Tuesday	Psalm 119:49-56
Wednesday	2 Corinthians 8:8-9
Thursday	Psalm 119: 9-16
Friday	Ecclesiastes 3:1-8
Saturday	Ecclesiastes 3:9-15

Week 30

Monday	Psalm 119:89-96
Tuesday	Proverbs 4:20-27
Wednesday	Philippians 1:3-6
Thursday	Isaiah 12:1-6
Friday	2 Timothy 1:12
Saturday	2 Corinthians 12:7-10

Week 31

Monday	2 Thessalonians 3:3-5
Tuesday	Job 1
Wednesday	Matthew 26:40-41
Thursday	Titus 3:1-8
Friday	Luke 6:37-42
Saturday	1 Peter 4:1-11

Week 32

Monday	Philippians 1:27
Tuesday	Ecclesiastes 5:1-7
Wednesday	Proverbs 1:10-19
Thursday	Judges 6:11-23
Friday	Titus 2:11-14
Saturday	Luke 12:6-7

Week 33

Monday	1 Peter 1:13-16
Tuesday	Psalm 35:1-3
Wednesday	Psalm 108:1-6
Thursday	1 Corinthians 10:12-13
Friday	2 Chronicles 14:8-11
Saturday	Psalm 119:33-40

Week 34

Monday	Psalm 89:13-18
Tuesday	Psalm 92
Wednesday	Galatians 2:19-21
Thursday	2 Corinthians 4:1-6
Friday	Proverbs 1:20-33
Saturday	Revelation 4:11

Week 35

Monday	James 1:12-17
Tuesday	Mark 3:23-27
Wednesday	Psalm 18:16-27
Thursday	Hebrews 2:14
Friday	Psalm 20
Saturday	1 Peter 2:1-3

Week 36

Monday	Psalm 17:1-9
Tuesday	Psalm 23
Wednesday	Job 2:1-10
Thursday	1 Corinthians 9:24-27
Friday	Ephesians 2:1-7
Saturday	Psalm 108:11-13

Week 37

Monday	Philippians 3:17-21
Tuesday	Acts 20:24
Wednesday	Psalm 107:9-15
Thursday	Psalm 40:6-8
Friday	Psalm 119:17-24
Saturday	1 Thessalonians 5:16-24

Week 38

Monday	2 Timothy 2:15
Tuesday	Psalm 119:57-64
Wednesday	James 3:13-18
Thursday	Hebrews 2:17-18
Friday	Psalm 37:3-5
Saturday	1 Corinthians 2:16

Week 39

Monday	2 Chronicles 7:14-16
Tuesday	Philippians 4:4-7
Wednesday	Psalm 60:11, 12
Thursday	2 Corinthians 5:14-15
Friday	Psalm 119:73-80
Saturday	2 Timothy 3:16-17

Week 40

Monday	Psalm 107:1-8
Tuesday	Ephesians 4:30
Wednesday	Proverbs 3:11-12
Thursday	1 John 2:1-6
Friday	John 8:37-47
Saturday	Mark 9:14-24

Week 41

Monday	Deuteronomy 5:32-33
Tuesday	Psalm 21:1-7
Wednesday	Luke 17:11-19
Thursday	James 5:13-17
Friday	Psalm 130
Saturday	2 Timothy 2:19-22

Week 42

Monday	1 Peter 2:4-12
Tuesday	Psalm 77:1-14
Wednesday	2 Peter 2:19
Thursday	Proverbs 7:1-4
Friday	1 John 4:1-4
Saturday	Psalm 19:7-14

Week 43

Monday	Psalm 119:1-8
Tuesday	Romans 12
Wednesday	James 1:2-8
Thursday	Deuteronomy 33:26-27
Friday	Job 5:8-17
Saturday	Psalm 85:7-8

Week 44

Monday	1 Peter 2:24-25
Tuesday	Proverbs 8:1-11
Wednesday	Psalm 107:17-21
Thursday	1 John 3:1-3
Friday	2 Chronicles 16:7-9a
Saturday	Psalm 139:21-24

Week 45

Monday	Ecclesiastes 12:13-14
Tuesday	Psalm 127:1-2
Wednesday	Proverbs 8:32-36
Thursday	Mark 7:14-23
Friday	Luke 12:15-21
Saturday	Ephesians 5:1-4

Week 46

Monday	Romans 1:16-25
Tuesday	Psalm 18:28-35
Wednesday	Proverbs 9:9-11
Thursday	Psalm 116:16-19
Friday	1 Corinthians 15:57-58
Saturday	Luke 12:22-31

Week 47

Monday	Romans 3:21-26
Tuesday	Romans 9:20-21
Wednesday	John 10:7-11
Thursday	Hebrews 4:15-16
Friday	2 Corinthians 11:2-3
Saturday	Genesis 3:1-13

Week 48

Monday	Psalm 121
Tuesday	Mark 8:34-38
Wednesday	Luke 18: 1-8
Thursday	Luke 18: 9-14
Friday	2 Timothy 1:7
Saturday	Ecclesiastes 9:10-12

Week 49

Monday	1 Peter 5:5-7
Tuesday	Romans 4:1-8
Wednesday	Deuteronomy 10:12-21
Thursday	2 Corinthians 6:3-10
Friday	Proverbs 21:2-3
Saturday	Luke 11:1-4 (NKJV)

Week 50

Monday	Exodus 3:1-14
Tuesday	Psalm 119:105-112
Wednesday	Exodus 15:1-6
Thursday	Psalm 24
Friday	1 Peter 1:3-9
Saturday	Exodus 20:1-17

Week 51

Monday	Psalm 119:25-32
Tuesday	Proverbs 3:1-8
Wednesday	1 Corinthians 1:18-25
Thursday	1 Corinthians 4:2
Friday	I Corinthians 1:26-31
Saturday	1 Corinthians 3:16-17

Week 52

Monday	Romans 6:1-7
Tuesday	Romans 6:5-14
Wednesday	Romans 6:15-23
Thursday	Romans 8:12-17
Friday	Romans 8:18-25
Saturday	Romans 8:31-39

Establishing a Weekly Battle Group Bible Study

Are you interested in starting a weekly *Winning the Battle of the Bulge* battle group in your church or home? It's easier than you think. The battle groups are formatted for a one-hour time slot, so they may fit in to a small group or Sunday School setting.

Here's what you will need:
- One person to facilitate thirteen weekly meetings.
- A *Winning the Battle of the Bulge* leader's packet.
- A *Winning the Battle of the Bulge* book and *Planning for the Battle of the Bulge* workbook/journal for each person attending the class.

The leader's packet and books are available through Looking Glass Ministries and will be discounted for groups of ten or more.

Mary is also available to speak and help motivate your group as you begin your Bible study. She has developed a one-day seminar to launch your battle group to assure that everyone will get the most out of their thirteen-week commitment. A training session for group leaders is also included.

To order books and learn more about starting a group contact:
Mary Englund Murphy
Looking Glass Ministries
10632 South Memorial Drive
Suite 126
Tulsa, OK 74133
918-254-2410
LookingGlassMinistries.com
Mary@LookingGlassMinistries.com

NOTES

NOTES

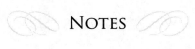

NOTES

NOTES